From Egg
to Bird

From Egg to Bird

Marlene Reidel

 Carolrhoda Books, Inc., Minneapolis

LIBRARY OF CONGRESS CATALOGING IN PUBLICATION DATA

Reidel, Marlene.
From egg to bird.

(A Carolrhoda start to finish book)
Ed. for 1973 published under title: Vom Nest zum
Vogel.
SUMMARY: Describes the development of a bird from
the time the egg is produced until the chick acquires
adult plumage.

1. Birds—Development—Juvenile literature. 2. Em-
bryology—Birds—Juvenile literature. [1. Birds—Devel-
opment] I. Title.

QL676.2.R4413   1981   598.2'3   81-56
ISBN 0-87614-159-9

2   3   4   5   6   7   8   9   10   86   85   84   83   82

From Egg to Bird

It is spring, and the trees are covered with blossoms.
This is the time of year when birds build their nests.
Here are two birds building a nest in a cherry tree.
One of the birds is a female and the other is a male.

After the birds mate,
the female lays her eggs in the nest.
She has laid three eggs this year.

After the birds mate,
the female lays her eggs in the nest.
She has laid three eggs this year.

In order to hatch, the eggs must be kept warm.

The two birds take turns warming the eggs.

They ruffle up their feathers and sit on the nest.

Inside each egg a baby bird is growing.

The thick yellow **yolk** provides food to help it grow.

The baby will grow until it fills up the whole egg.

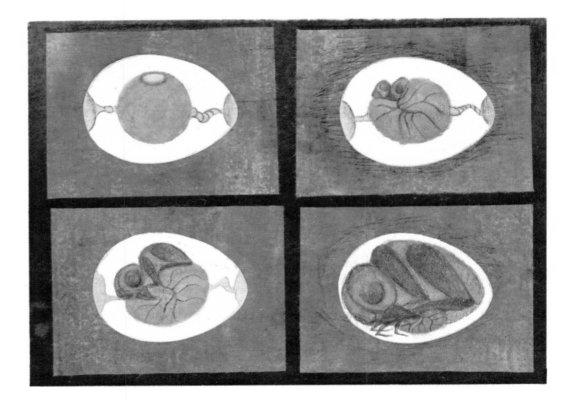

In about three weeks
a baby is ready to hatch.
It pecks at the egg shell
until it breaks open a space
large enough to fit through.
When baby birds hatch out of their shells,
they are wet and cold.
So the parents keep them warm
by covering the babies with their own bodies.

Soon the baby birds are dry.
They are covered with soft,
fluffy feathers called **down**.
They open their beaks and chirp for food.
The parents gather insects and worms
and feed them to the babies.

The baby birds grow fast.
Soon they lose their down
and grow strong adult feathers.
As soon as they have their adult feathers,
the babies learn how to fly.

Now it is autumn,
and the weather is turning cold.
Many birds are flying south
where the weather is warmer.
Our bird family joins them.
They will go south for the winter.
But they will be back in the spring
when the weather here becomes warmer
and the blossoms cover the trees again.

**Marlene
Reidel**

MARLENE REIDEL was born in lower Bavaria and was raised on an isolated farm called *Krottenthal.* She is the oldest of seven children.

Ms. Reidel studied ceramics as a girl and then went on to attend the Academy of Fine Arts in Munich. She has written and illustrated many children's books and has received numerous honors and awards for her work, including the German Youth Book Prize, the Most Beautiful German Book of the Year award, the Culture Prize of Eastern Bavaria, and the Special Prize of the German Academy for Children's and Youth Literature.

THE CAROLRHODA
>>> START

From Beet to Sugar

From Blossom to Honey

From Cacao Bean to Chocolate

From Cement to Bridge

From Clay to Bricks

From Cotton to Pants

From Cow to Shoe

From Dinosaurs to Fossils

From Egg to Bird

From Egg to Butterfly

From Fruit to Jam

From Grain to Bread

From Grass to Butter

From Ice to Rain

From Milk to ice Cream

From Oil to Gasoline

From Ore to Spoon

From Sand to Glass

From Seed to Pear

From Sheep to Scarf

From Tree to Table

TO FINISH >>>

BOOKS